John Brian Losh Presents
THE LEGENDS OF LUXURY REAL ESTATE
VOLUME II

First published in 2006 by Luxury Real Estate
2110 Western Avenue, Seattle, WA 98121
800.488.4066
www.LuxuryRealEstate.com

All rights reserved. No portion of this publication may be reproduced in any manner whatsoever
without permission in writing from Luxury Real Estate.

Executive Vice President: Matthew Haber
Managing Editor: Jennifer Schaefer | **Publications Manager:** Courtney Jackson
Art Direction: James Short, Antoine Do | **Graphic Design:** Ashley Ernst

Photo Credits
Page 1: Courtesy of Ewing & Clark, Inc.; photographed by Jason LeMoine
Page 4: Courtesy of Willis Allen Real Estate; photographed by Roberto Zebellos
Page 6: Courtesy of John Daugherty, Realtors

Copyright © 2006 by Luxury Real Estate
A DIVISION OF JOHN BRIAN LOSH, INC.

ISBN: 1-886020-16-7

PRINTED IN THE U.S.A.

John Brian Losh Presents

THE LEGENDS OF
LUXURY REAL ESTATE

VOLUME II

Published by Luxury Real Estate
A DIVISION OF JOHN BRIAN LOSH, INC.

LUXURY
REAL ESTATE
LUXURYREALESTATE.COM

CONTENTS

Forward

In 2005 I was privileged to publish Volume I of *The Legends of Luxury Real Estate*. As Chairman of the Luxury Real Estate network I am keenly aware of the many extraordinary accomplishments of our 1,000+ members. They are simply stated, the best of the best in the industry, combining years of experience, proven expertise, discretion and 5-star customer service.

I am pleased to present *The Legends of Luxury Real Estate: Volume II*. On the following pages, you will get a glimpse into the lives and careers of 27 legendary real estate brokers and the properties they represent. The featured brokers include New Orleans-based Eleanor Farnsworth, who persevered through Hurricane Katrina and grew stronger for it, as well as Elizabeth Stribling of Stribling & Associates in Manhattan, the exclusive sales agent for the transformation of the world-famous Plaza Hotel into residential condominiums. Also profiled are Robbie Briggs and Charles Freeman, top brokers responsible for merging two of the oldest and most respected Dallas real estate companies, and Carolyn V. Klemm, an accomplished fashion buyer and designer who became Litchfield County's leading broker of country estates.

For an always current look at these brokers' listings, as well as those of their colleagues, I invite you to visit the most-viewed luxury real estate Web site in the world, LuxuryRealEstate.com. Enjoy!

John Brian Losh
CEO/Publisher

{ THE 1,000-PLUS BROKERS IN OUR NETWORK ARE TRULY THE BEST OF THE BEST IN THE LUXURY REAL ESTATE INDUSTRY. }

{ ${L}$ITCHFIELD COUNTY HAS A DISTINCTLY COUNTRY FEEL, with rolling hills, pristine lakes and lots of land trusts. Residents enjoy the best of two worlds in that the area is situated less than a two-hour drive from New York and less than a three-hour drive from Boston. The charm and quality of life Litchfield County offers is rarely found so close to major metropolitan areas. Many of the area's historic properties have been preserved, so driving through this part of the country is a treat. }

Antique Colonial overlooking Shepaug River

KLEMM REAL ESTATE

Klemm Real Estate is the No. 1 seller of fine real estate in Litchfield County. Over the past 20 years, Klemm Real Estate has built a reputation both nationally and internationally as the No. 1 leader of luxury property sales and marketing throughout Litchfield County, serving all 26 towns and villages from the company's four offices. Klemm Real Estate has been selected Best American Estate Agency in the International Property Awards sponsored by the *Wall Street Journal* and Bentley Motors.

KLEMM REAL ESTATE
6 Titus Road, P.O. Box 396
Washington Depot, CT 06794

TEL | 860.868.7313
FAX | 860.868.9139
E-MAIL | carolyn@klemmrealestate.com
WEB SITE | www.klemmrealestate.com

Carolyn V. Klemm
Litchfield County, Connecticut

About Carolyn V. Klemm

Born in London, Carolyn moved to Scarsdale, New York with her family at the age of 9. As an adult, she worked as a buyer and fashion designer at Lord & Taylor, Saks Fifth Avenue and Bergdorf Goodman and managed a dozen boutiques from New York to Chicago. Thirty years ago, she and her husband decided to move to Connecticut to expose their two sons to a more rural way of life. Carolyn chose a career in real estate because the flexibility suited her lifestyle.

Throughout her career, Carolyn has worked with many luminary clients, including Ivan Lendl, Michael J. Fox, Tom Browkaw and Henry Kissinger—some of whom may not have chosen to live in Litchfield County were it not for her encouragement. She has sold the historic Mayflower Inn three times and has witnessed its transformation into a wonderful relais and châteaux. She has also encouraged clients to donate land to trusts to ensure perpetual protection of the area she and her family call home.

A DISTINCTLY
country feel

[OPPOSITE] Private Litchfield County Compound in Goshen, Connecticut [TOP LEFT] One of New England's most spectacular and unique properties overlooking Lake Waramaug with exquisite & majestic views from every room [TOP RIGHT] Completely restored 4,500 square foot Colonial located in Bridgewater, Connecticut

[ABOVE] Shingle-style main residence with carriage house and guest apartment, pool, pool house and 11-car garaging [RIGHT] Colonial Post Office in Litchfield, Connecticut, where the second floor is the location of Klemm Real Estate's Litchfield office

{ *N*EWPORT IS KNOWN FOR ITS MILES OF SCENIC COASTLINE, IDEAL FOR EXHILARATING SAILING EXCURSIONS, RELAXING BEACH TIME AND REJUVENATING WALKS, as well as its opulent historic homes. Residences built in the 18th and 19th centuries have undergone painstaking renovations to preserve the original architectural details while incorporating today's modern conveniences. Many of Newport's mansions, or "summer cottages" as they are called, are open for daily tours. }

GUSTAVE WHITE SOTHEBY'S INTERNATIONAL REALTY

Gustave White Sotheby's International Realty has been the leader in the Newport luxury market since 1925. The company's experienced staff offers personalized and professional real estate service to all residential buyers and sellers. In the past decade, Gustave White Sotheby's International Realty has grown from 8 to 28 agents and from $11 million in sales to just over $200 million, while maintaining the high standards of professionalism and integrity for which the firm has always been recognized. In 2005, the company added a second office in Westerly, Rhode Island.

GUSTAVE WHITE SOTHEBY'S INTERNATIONAL REALTY

37 Bellevue Avenue
Newport, RI 02840

TEL | 401.849.3000
FAX | 401.849.9310
E-MAIL | cwest@gustavewhite.com
E-MAIL | pleys@gustavewhite.com
WEB SITE | www.gustavewhite.com

Chris West & Paul Leys
Newport, Rhode Island

About Chris West & Paul Leys

After earning a degree in education from Bucknell University, Chris chose a career in real estate, earning her license in 1983. She worked for another local agency until joining Gustave J.S. White Real Estate in 1994 as managing broker. In 2000 she and Paul Leys bought the agency. Chris is a past chair of the Newport County Board of Realtor's Grievance committee. She is married with three children and five grandchildren.

Paul was born and raised in Newport and graduated from Providence College in 1983. While earning his real estate license in 1988, he followed his dad's advice and talked to Francis "Gerry" Dwyer, owner/broker of Gustave J.S. White Real Estate at the time. He has been at the company ever since. Active in the real estate community, in 1999 he was voted by his peers as Newport County Realtor of the Year. At present, he is the Rhode Island Association's Treasurer. He lives in Newport with his wife Mardie and five children.

Paul Leys (left) and Chris West

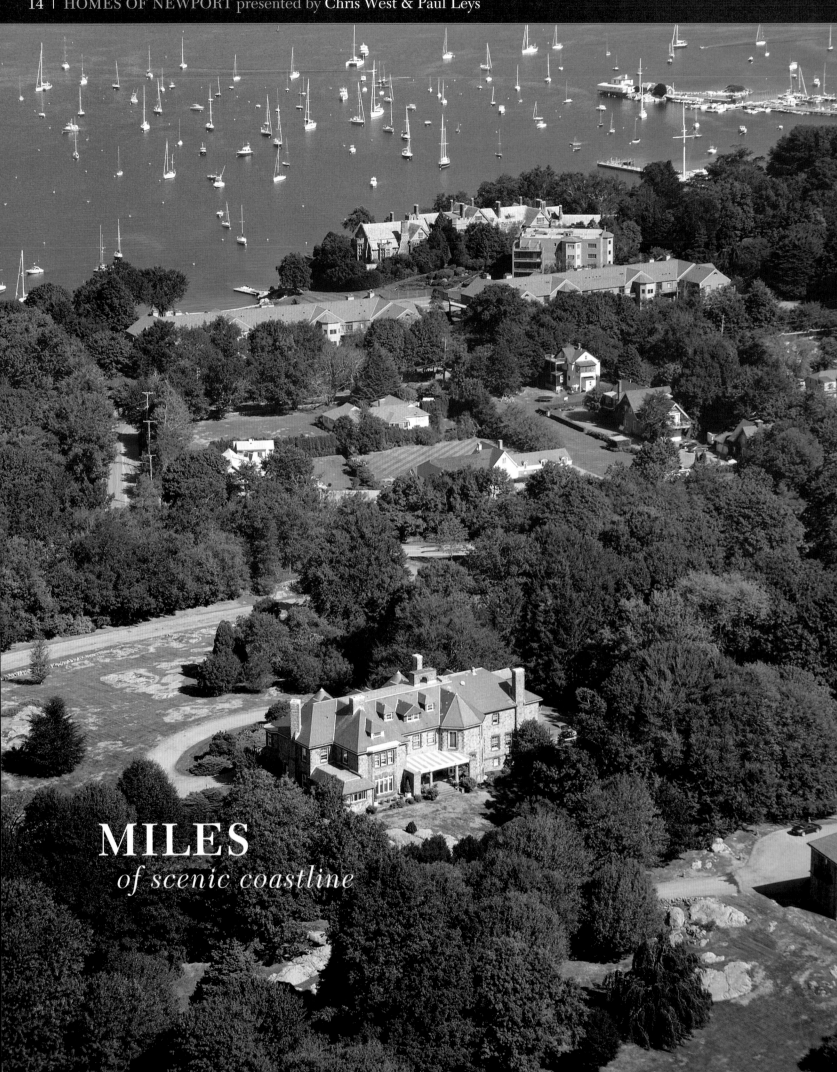

MILES
of scenic coastline

company
Gustave White Sotheby's
International Realty

title
Brokers/co-owners

years in business:
Chris: 23, Paul: 18

area of expertise
Coastal Rhode Island into
neighboring Connecticut and
Massachusetts, specializing in
Newport County and Watch Hill

interests
Chris: Family and friends;
water and beach activities,
including sailing

Paul: Ice hockey, snowboarding,
volunteering for youth
organizations

[OPPOSITE] Roslyn, a baronial stone estate with Newport Harbor in the distance [TOP LEFT] A shingle-style Victorian contemporary on Ocean Drive overlooking the Atlantic Ocean [TOP RIGHT] A Victorian library on Newport's famed Bellevue Avenue

[ABOVE] A gourmet kitchen with spectacular Sakonnet Passage water views in Portsmouth, Rhode Island [MIDDLE RIGHT] An adorable Portsmouth waterfront getaway [BOTTOM RIGHT] A stylish, meticulously renovated 1864 Victorian villa designed by George Champlin Mason

All photography by John Corbett

FRANKLIN LAKES IS A BOROUGH LOCATED IN BERGEN COUNTY, NEW JERSEY, LESS THAN 20 MILES FROM NEW YORK CITY, which is home to about 12,000 residents. Recognized as "one of the richest places to live in North America," Franklin Lakes boasts many stunning multimillion-dollar mansions with beautifully manicured landscaping. The area offers a wide variety of attractions, including country parks, golf courses and historic sites from the 18th, 19th and 20th centuries.

Franklin Lakes Indian Trail Club's new clubhouse

MCBRIDE AGENCY REALTOR

McBride Agency Realtor started as a subsidiary of McBride Enterprises. The company was founded by J. Nevins McBride in 1960. To date, McBride has developed over 1,200 building lots in Franklin Lakes. The company is the founder of Urban Farms, New Jersey's finest club community, where residents enjoy custom-built homes situated on hundreds of acres of woodland circling a magnificent lake, a private country club and a golf club. McBride markets homes in Franklin Lakes and the surrounding communities.

MCBRIDE AGENCY REALTOR
834 Franklin Lake Rd.
Franklin Lakes, NJ 07417

TEL | 201.891.8900
FAX | 201.891.7758
E-MAIL | office@mcbrideagency.com
WEB SITE | www.mcbrideagency.com

W. Peter McBride
Franklin Lakes, New Jersey

About W. Peter McBride

Peter, a second-generation real estate professional who is the son of J. Nevins McBride, carries on the entrepreneurial spirit and leadership that launched McBride Agency Realtor nearly 50 years ago. He is the president and chief operating officer of two family-held businesses: McBride Enterprises, Inc. and Urban Farms, Inc. McBride Enterprises, Inc. is a real estate and development company. Urban Farms, Inc. is the residential development company responsible for growing the Urban Farms community, which was first developed more than 30 years ago. Founded with the goal of creating a family environment that is synonymous with excellence, today Urban Farms offers more than 800 families a safe and tranquil community that is convenient to transportation and major shopping centers. Peter is also president of the Indian Trail Club, a tennis and swim club on Franklin Lake with 550 members. Peter also serves as a trustee of New Jersey's Ramapo College. Peter and his wife Pam, an architect, are active with Habitat for Humanity, Paterson, New Jersey.

STUNNING
multimillion-dollar mansions

[OPPOSITE] Windover Chateau – Experience the fine details of true craftsmanship and design as you enter this prestigious estate
[TOP LEFT] Charming Franklin Lakes estate [TOP RIGHT] Solid luxury

[ABOVE] A true masterpeice [MIDDLE RIGHT] A grand Franklin Lakes estate
[BOTTOM RIGHT] Elegant Georgian colonial

{ *O*NLY AN HOUR AND A HALF FROM MANHATTAN, THE DELAWARE RIVER VALLEY IS A QUIET PLACE, CONTENT UNTO ITSELF. Social life centers around quiet walks in the country, small dinner parties, lovely restaurants hidden in the countryside and evenings spent in front of the fire. Tennis courts, riding stables, boating on the Delaware, cross-country skiing and outstanding golf clubs are available for sports enthusiasts. Great fun, too, are the many antique shops and art galleries, farmers markets and flea markets. }

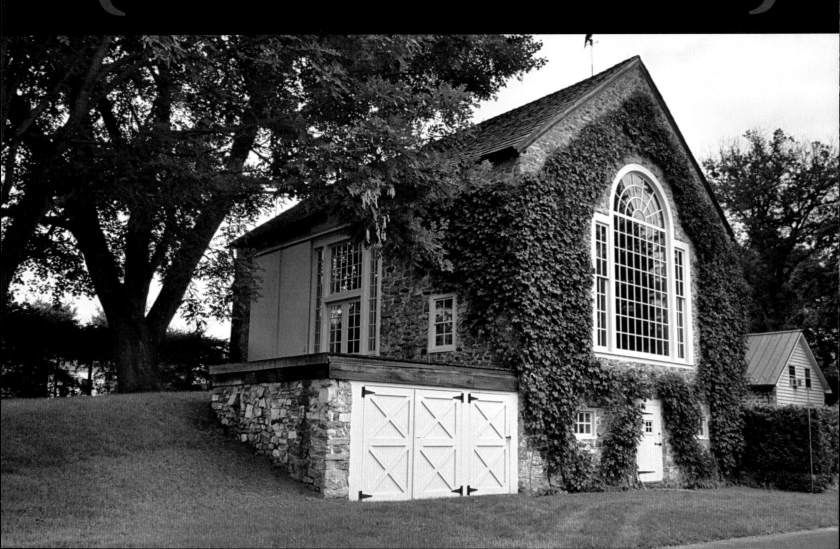

LISA JAMES OTTO COUNTRY PROPERTIES

Lisa James Otto Country Properties is a boutique real estate firm by the river's edge with offices in New Hope and Doylestown, Pennsylvania, as well as Stockton, New Jersey. The company specializes in antique historic houses, charming country houses, farms and estates and riverfront cottages. Lisa James Otto Country Properties has a horse farms international division, as well as a commercial division. Recent additions include a title company and a restoration and interior design company.

**LISA JAMES OTTO
COUNTRY PROPERTIES**
One South Sugan Road
New Hope, PA 18938

TEL | 215.862.2626
FAX | 215.862.2666
E-MAIL | ljo@lisajamesotto.com
WEB SITE | www.lisajamesotto.com

Lisa James Otto
Bucks County, Pennsylvania

About Lisa James Otto

After obtaining a degree in German and French at Boston University and University of Vienna in Austria and working at Hermès in Paris, Lisa returned to her native Bucks County to work in her mother's and her father's real estate firms. Her mother, Elizabeth James, was known for her advertising acumen, fine intellect and tremendous sense of humor and was a brilliant negotiator. Her father, Wynne James, Jr., a second-generation real estate broker, was known for his wit, keen negotiating skills and kindness.

Lisa created her own real estate company in 1986 after her parents passed away. Her client portfolio quickly spread from a loyal following of young investment bankers to models, actors and film producers who wanted to find a quiet country place.

In 1986, Lisa joined the New York Council of FIABCI, the International Real Estate Federation based in Paris, of which she has been president for the last three years.

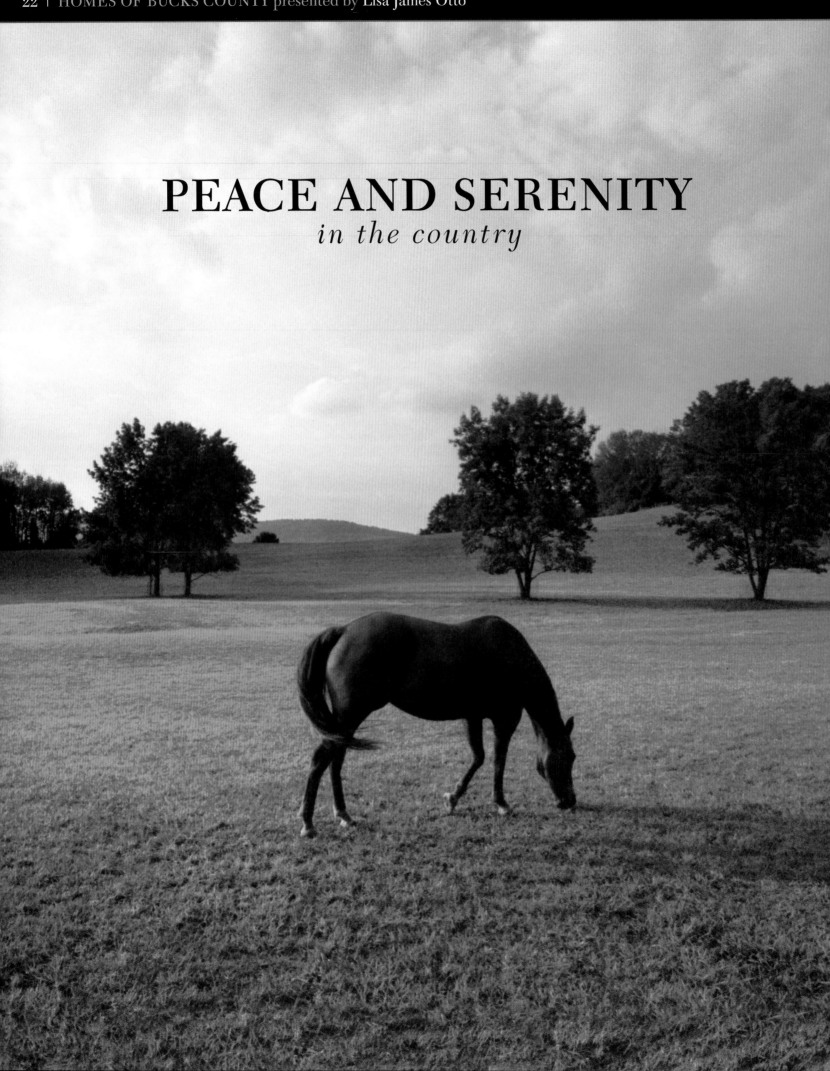

PEACE AND SERENITY
in the country

company
Lisa James Otto Country Properties

title
Founder, president and CEO

years in business: 35

area of expertise
Bucks, Montgomery and Hunterdon Counties, farms, estates, country houses, historic fieldstone homes, riverfront properties, horse facilities and investment properties

interests
Family, sailing, farm and land preservation, international travel, international real estate, interior design and restoration

[OPPOSITE] A magnificent horse farm with endless panoramic views [TOP LEFT] A historic fieldstone home on 30 majestic acres overlooking the Panacaussing Creek [TOP RIGHT] Rolling green pastures and fields convey the tranquility that is Bucks County, Pennsylvania

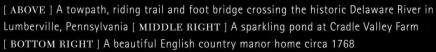

[ABOVE] A towpath, riding trail and foot bridge crossing the historic Delaware River in Lumberville, Pennsylvania [MIDDLE RIGHT] A sparkling pond at Cradle Valley Farm
[BOTTOM RIGHT] A beautiful English country manor home circa 1768

NEW YORK IS THE MOST VIBRANT CITY IN THE WORLD, AND ITS ENERGY IS INFECTIOUS, attracting some of the world's most dynamic people and drawing millions of tourists a year. Beyond the obvious landmarks, including Central Park, the Empire State Building, Times Square and the Statue of Liberty, there are beautiful sights around every corner—from towering skyscrapers to quaint townhouses to ornate architectural landmarks to unexpected pockets of greenery and flowers.

STRIBLING & ASSOCIATES

Stribling & Associates is one of the most highly regarded residential real estate firms in New York. With three offices, the company specializes in premium properties on the Upper East and West Sides, as well as downtown. A high percentage of Stribling's associates have worked for more than 20 years in the business and are well-known and respected by both the real estate community and home buyers and sellers for their expertise. Many consider Stribling to be the standard by which others are judged.

STRIBLING & ASSOCIATES
942 Madison Avenue
New York, NY 10024

TEL | 212.570.2440
FAX | 212.570.0138
E-MAIL | estribling@stribling.com
WEB SITE | www.stribling.com

Elizabeth Stribling
New York, New York

About Elizabeth Stribling

Elizabeth moved to New York from Georgia with her parents at the age of 7. After studying literature and the modern novel as a college student, she decided to pursue a career in luxury real estate when the idea was proposed to her at a gala ball held at one of Newport, Rhode Island's legendary palatial homes. Beginning as a rookie real estate broker in 1967, she went on to establish Stribling & Associates in 1980. In the 1990s, she began working in the international property marketplace, and by the end of the decade she had established a property development marketing division, Stribling Marketing Associates.

Throughout her career, Elizabeth has had many notable transactions, an example being the sale of the Robert Lehman mansion on West 54th Street in the mid-1970s, which led to the Robert Lehman wing of the Metropolitan Museum of Art. More recently, Stribling & Associates was appointed the exclusive sales agent for the transformation of the world-famous Plaza Hotel into residential condominiums.

THE MOST
vibrant city in the world

company
Stribling & Associates

title
President

years in business: 39

area of expertise
Manhattan and Brooklyn

interests
Historic preservation, foreign affairs, theater, culinary arts

[OPPOSITE] The Private Residences at the iconic Plaza Hotel [TOP LEFT] An elegant formal dining room designed by James K. Pine in the Stillman House [TOP RIGHT] A classic prewar cooperative apartment

[ABOVE] An impressive townhouse drawing room featuring an ornate Italian-hung plaster ceiling [RIGHT] A sweeping staircase designed by Catherine Stevens Associates in an Upper East Side mansion

THE HISTORIC VILLAGE OF MIDDLEBURG WAS ESTABLISHED IN 1787 BY REVOLUTIONARY WAR LIEUTENANT COLONEL and Virginia statesman Levin Powell. The legacy of the Colonial era continues today at Middleburg's many charming inns, shops and restaurants, some of which date back to the town's earliest days. With a population of just over 600 residents, Middleburg has earned a reputation as the Nation's Horse and Hunt Capital, attracting prominent visitors from across the U.S.

THOMAS & TALBOT REAL ESTATE

Established in 1967, Thomas & Talbot Real Estate is a small, efficient and effective firm with more than 250 years of combined sales experience. The company specializes in the brokerage of high-end country estates and agricultural properties in Loudoun County, the adjacent Virginia counties of Fauquier, Clarke and Rappahannock, and beyond. Thomas & Talbot's continued success is in large part due to the company's full-time staff of award-winning, dedicated agents.

THOMAS & TALBOT
REAL ESTATE
2 South Madison Street
Middleburg, VA 20117

TEL | 540.687.6500
FAX | 540.687.8899
E-MAIL | info@thomasandtalbot.com
WEB SITE | www.thomas-talbot.com

Phillip S. Thomas
Middleburg, Virginia

About Phillip S. Thomas

A fifth-generation resident of Loudoun County, Phillip has been involved in the hunt country of Northern Virginia all his life. A Loudoun County landowner since 1962, he chose a career in country real estate in part for the opportunity to create a local business. Phillip founded Thomas & Talbot Real Estate in 1967.

A staunch supporter of land easements, Phillip has never knowingly sold a property for development. He was the recipient of the Piedmont Environmental Council Land Conservation Award in 2001. Thomas & Talbot states its philosophy on the back of the company's annual steeplechase calendar: "It is our firm's continued philosophy to help maintain the open spaces and agricultural integrity of this beautiful and unique area."

A longtime activist in the Loudoun County community, Phillip is a former director of the Goose Creek Association, which represents local citizens interested in protecting the natural resources, historic heritage and quality of life in their rural community.

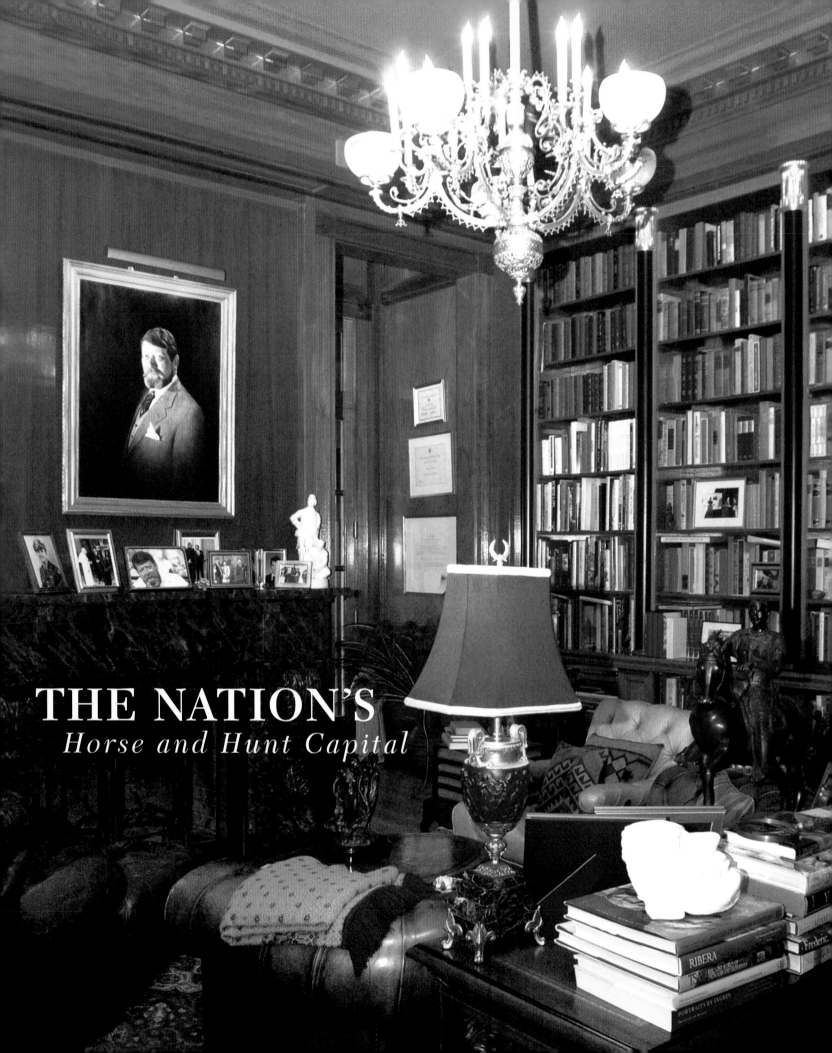

THE NATION'S
Horse and Hunt Capital

company
Thomas & Talbot Real Estate

title
Founder/owner

years in business: 39

area of expertise
Farms and estates in the
Piedmont area of Virgina

interests
Landscape design, sporting art
collections and restoration of
period homes

[OPPOSITE] The beautiful library of the home pictured top left with doors opening to the porch, mahogany paneling, floor-to-ceiling shelving and ebonized and gilded columns [TOP LEFT] A magnificent manor on 245 acres of high rolling land [TOP RIGHT] Ballroom of Chesley Manor pictured left

[ABOVE] New England country house overlooking a 10 acre lake on 167 acre estate
[MIDDLE RIGHT] Ten acre lake of country estate located in the foothills of Blue Ridge Mountains [BOTTOM RIGHT] Dining room of Lakeview country estate with view of the mountains

ORT LAUDERDALE HAS A STYLE ALL ITS OWN—FRESH AND LIVELY, YET SOPHISTICATED. Long known for its beautiful beaches, miles of waterways and sunny weather, today the city also boasts a great number of five-star hotels and luxury beach and city condominiums. Fort Lauderdale is the undisputed home of the world's mega-yachts, which delight the eyes as they travel the Intercoastal or nestle beside waterfront homes.

INTERCOASTAL REALTY

Family owned and operated for over 25 years, Intercoastal Realty is a boutique-style company with a stellar reputation within the Fort Lauderdale community. Intercoastal Realty's experienced team of real estate professionals are based out of a single office, where they create a synergy that consistently makes the company the undisputed leader in the listing and selling of waterfront and luxury homes in Fort Lauderdale.

INTERCOASTAL REALTY
1500 East Las Olas Boulevard
Fort Lauderdale, FL 33301

TEL | 954.525.7528
FAX | 954.467.6714
E-MAIL | beth@intercoastalrealty.com
WEB SITE | www.intercoastalrealty.com

Beth Beauchamp
Fort Lauderdale, Florida

About Beth Beauchamp

After 27 satisfying years of managing a home and raising three sons, Beth decided to try a new career in real estate with the enthusiastic support of her husband, Jack. That was the beginning of what has become a thriving business that the whole family enjoys.

Beth bought Intercoastal Realty in 1980 and set about changing it into a "waterfront-only" brokerage—a good decision, as the company prospered and became a household name in Fort Lauderdale. Then, as property values rose dramatically, it became evi-

dent to Beth that the company needed to expand its focus from waterfront properties only, to include non-waterfront properties in order to list more affordable homes. That, too, proved to be a successful move as Fort Lauderdale continues to be an international destination of choice.

Over the years, Beth has refused to entertain offers to buy Intercoastal Realty or to merge it with another company. Intercoastal still operates out of one office, earning a third of a billion dollars in sales in 2005.

FRESH AND LIVELY,
yet sophisticated

company
Intercoastal Realty

title
President/owner

years in business: 28

area of expertise
Fort Lauderdale coastal
properties, specializing in
luxury waterfront

interests
Family gatherings, reading,
walking, water exercise

[OPPOSITE] A Premier Point estate with wide water views and deep dockage for almost any size yacht [TOP LEFT] A resort-style pool at a lavish family home [TOP RIGHT] The western view from the Intracoastal Waterway along the New River to Fort Lauderdale

[ABOVE] A luxury condominium with great spaces and downtown skyline and Intracoastal

{ *N*APLES IS A POPULAR DESTINATION FOR BOTH U.S. AND FOREIGN VISITORS. The sub-tropical climate and miles of white sandy beaches make the city a perfect getaway location and winter resting place. Naples' population during the off-season is around 21,000, but swells to more than 36,000 when the winter residents and visitors arrive. The city is well prepared to handle the influx, with a wealth of wonderful lodging, dining, shopping and sightseeing options. }

BARRY DENICOLA REALTY

Barry DeNicola Realty is all about family. Currently working at the company are Barry's four daughters, his son and three son-in-laws and they all are either licensed realtors or brokers. The dedication and level of service for their clients is second to none in the industry, offering the latest technology for displaying and marketing each client's properties. Barry specializes in waterfront and golf properties in the Naples/Barefoot Beach/Bonita Springs areas, providing confidential, discrete and thorough buyer representation. As a longtime resident of Barefoot Beach Barry's knowledge of Gulf of Mexico properties and waterfront boating properties is extensive, ranging from single-family homes to villas to high-rise and mid-size condominiums.

BARRY DENICOLA REALTY
4892 Bonita Beach Road
Bonita Springs, FL 34134

TEL | 239.947.6111
FAX | 239.947.3006
E-MAIL | barrycdenicola@aol.com
WEB SITE | www.barrycdenicola.com

Barry DeNicola
Naples, Florida

About Barry DeNicola

Barry DeNicola meets the residential real estate needs of some of Florida's most coveted areas, representing luxury properties that range from $1 million to more than $10 million. He operates out of his single office in Bonita Springs which sits on a wide pristine bay just several hundred yards from the beach.

Barry has been a member of Luxury Real Estate since 2002 and established his own real estate business in 2003—the crown on a vibrant and successful career. He is also affiliated with Leading Estates of the World, FIABCI, NAR/International and Unique Homes.

In 2005, Barry exceeded $250 million in closed sales, and his combined sales volume for the past three years is well over $550 million. He was previously ranked the 24th real estate specialist in the U.S. and the No. 1 real estate specialist in the state of Florida by the National Association of Realtors.

THE PERFECT
getaway location

company
Barry DeNicola Realty

title
Owner/broker

years in business: 7

area of expertise
Gulf of Mexico, bay, canal and riverfront single family homes and sites, condominiums and

villas, as well as certain golf course communities in Naples, Barefoot Beach, Bonita Springs and Bonita Beach areas. Properties valued from $1 to $10 million+

interests
Caring for over 100 monkeys at a primate sanctuary with wife Toni, as well as 5 monkeys in a rainforest environment at their

beach home, President of Florida Simiam Society, boating, fishing and relaxing on beautiful Barefoot Beach with kids and grandchildren

[OPPOSITE] The Naples Pier — The most popular gathering place in Naples [TOP LEFT] A beautiful 4 story Mediterranean home on beautiful Barefoot Beach in North Naples [TOP RIGHT] This 3 story home with elevated pool offers picturesque sunsets over Bonita Beach

[ABOVE] A Mediterranean estate home located in Quail West — Naples/Bonita Springs premier golf community [MIDDLE RIGHT] Barefoot Bay home — Turnkey furnished 3 & 4 story homes overlooking the bay and gulf [BOTTOM RIGHT] Bonita Beach lot with tropical palms and white powder sand

{ *N*EW ORLEANS COMBINES OLD WORLD HERITAGE WITH A VIBRANT MODERN LIFESTYLE. This balance is best reflected in the oldest neighborhoods, where homes exhibit European architecture against the backdrop of a tropical landscape. It is here that jazz was born, Mardi Gras kings first reigned and the motto emerged, *"Laissez les bons temps roulers!"* (Let the good times roll!) In the wake of Hurricane Katrina, New Orleans continues to recreate itself, upheld by rich traditions in music, cuisine and art. }

PRUDENTIAL GARDNER, REALTORS

With deep roots in the New Orleans area that date back to 1943, Prudential Gardner, Realtors has grown to be the leading broker in the Southeast Louisiana and Southern Mississippi region with a network of 25 offices that serve more than 100 communities. The company was ranked as the 52nd largest real estate company in the nation and the 9th largest Prudential affiliate in the May 2004 issue of *Real Trends* magazine.

ELEANOR FARNSWORTH
CRS, GRI, BRC
HISTORIC RESIDENTIAL SPECIALIST
Prudential Gardner, Realtors
2727 Prytania Street, Suite 15
New Orleans, Louisiana 70130

TEL | 504.891.1142
FAX | 504.891.1148
E-MAIL | sold@eleanorfarnsworth.com
WEB SITE | www.eleanorfarnsworth.com

Eleanor Farnsworth
New Orleans, Louisiana

About Eleanor Farnsworth

Eleanor has been a key figure in the revitalization of her beloved city. She is a preservationist in the truest sense of the word, having applied her expertise in historic residential sales to restore ownership in the city's most sought-after neighborhoods, including the Garden District, Uptown, University, French Quarter and the Warehouse District.

A two-time winner of New Orleans' prestigious Diamond Award for highest sales volume, Eleanor attributes her 26 years of success to an aggressive and customized marketing approach. Clients find her engaging personality, wit and lifetime relationship with the city to be a crucial asset in the specialized market of New Orleans' historic luxury real estate market.

A dedicated community servant, Eleanor has directed her talents to the Preservation Resource Center and serves as a fellow for the New Orleans Museum of Art. She is a member of the Junior League Interior Decorating and Gardening Clubs. Her diverse involvement and career experience have earned her recognition as a YWCA role model.

THE OPULENCE
of ages past revived

company
Prudential Gardner, Realtors

title
Realtor, Historic Residential
Specialist

years in business: 26

interests
Family, preservation, travel, art
and antiques

area of expertise
Luxury sales in New Orleans'
historic neighborhoods, including the Garden District, Uptown,
University, French Quarter and
the Warehouse District

[OPPOSITE] A grand ballroom, richly imbued with gilded accents [TOP LEFT] New Orleans' beloved "Wedding Cake" house, graced with ornate classical moldings, Corinthian columns and heavenly spires [TOP RIGHT] Elegant Victorian home on prestigious oak-lined St. Charles Avenue

[ABOVE] "Uptown's Versailles" custom-built in majestic 18th century French style

[RIGHT] Lush tropical plants, sculptures and a jewel-toned pool adorn a lavish slate courtyard

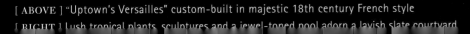

PALM BEACH IS A WORLD-FAMOUS RESORT COMMUNITY OFFERING A LIFESTYLE ON A GRAND SCALE. Although Palm Beach is home to many rich and famous people, the town's hospitality to visitors is unmatched. The finest hotels, gourmet restaurants, exquisite beaches and the incomparable shopping of the legendary Worth Avenue are just a few of the amenities. Living in Palm Beach gives one an opportunity to be a part of one of the finest and friendliness communities in the world.

WILSHIRE INTERNATIONAL REALTY CO.

For more than 25 years, Wilshire International Realty Co., a widely recognized real estate company in the Palm Beaches, has specialized in the sale of commercial and luxury residential properties in the multimillions of dollars. Wilshire International Realty Co. is known for providing outstanding service to both domestic and international clients looking to buy or sell commercial or luxury real estate.

WILSHIRE INTERNATIONAL
REALTY CO.
125 Worth Avenue
Palm Beach, FL 33480

TEL | 561.835.8001
FAX | 561.835.8002
E-MAIL | cafranks@bellsouth.net
WEB SITE | www.WilshirePalmBeach.com

Christine Franks
Palm Beach, Florida

About Christine Franks

After earning two college degrees, Christine joined the ranks of the real estate industry 25 years ago, when her husband, who has worked in real estate for 40-plus years, asked her to join him. This led to her working exclusively in Palm Beach, where they make their home.

At Wilshire International Realty Co., Christine oversees a full-service staff of experienced multilingual associates using the most modern technology. She is a past president of the Palm Beach Board of Realtors and a past president and chairperson of the Greater South Country Road Association beautification of Palm Beach.

Christine is passionate about the prestigious area in which she lives. Lending frequent support to local charities and community services, she is a respected figure in her community.

A WORLD-FAMOUS
resort community

company
Wilshire International Realty Co.

title
President/broker/owner

years in business: 25

area of expertise
Palm Beach residential and
commercial real estate

interests
Spending time with family,
reading and creative writing,
visual arts, architectural
design, community and charitable
involvement, travel

[OPPOSITE] Villa de Monaco, a superb oceanfront estate with private beachside terrace [TOP LEFT] Exceptional interior design with the finest appointment and craftsmanship [TOP RIGHT] Palm Beach outdoor luxury living for year-round entertainment and enjoyment with privacy and security

[ABOVE] Architectural Mizner-style masterpiece [MIDDLE RIGHT] A superb master suite overlooking lush tropical gardens and the inviting pool and spa [BOTTOM RIGHT] Town Hall overlooking the Memorial Fountain in the heart of Palm Beach

*A*TLANTA'S VARIETY OF CULTURAL ACTIVITIES, ARCHITECTURE AND COMMERCE, combined with Georgians' genuine Southern hospitality, make the city a diverse and enjoyable place to live. Although Atlanta is well-known for its history, the present paints an equally vivid picture. The city has grown from a small town to a metropolis with more than 400,000 residents, a new ballpark, a revitalized midtown and neighborhoods linked to the city center.

JENNY PRUITT & ASSOCIATES, REALTORS

Established in 1988, Jenny Pruitt & Associates, Realtors specializes in prestigious properties located throughout metro Atlanta. Offering expert service in every aspect of residential real estate, the company also offers a nationally acclaimed Relocation Department. Jenny Pruitt & Associates, Realtors is ranked among the Top 100 Brokers in the U.S. by REAL Trends, an industry-tracking organization endorsed by the National Association of Realtors and the Real Estate Brokerage Managers Council.

**JENNY PRUITT &
ASSOCIATES, REALTORS**
990 Hammond Drive, Suite 300
Atlanta, GA 30328

TEL | 770.394.5400
FAX | 770.399.3022
E-MAIL | jenny@jennypruitt.com
WEB SITE | www.jennypruitt.com

Jenny Pruitt
Atlanta, Georgia

About Jenny Pruitt

A lifelong resident of Atlanta, Jenny began her career as an agent with a well-respected company in her hometown and was soon promoted to vice president/managing broker. A shrewd business acumen and dedication to treating clients the way she likes to be treated made her into an overnight success. In 1980, Jenny was named Atlanta's Realtor of the Year, and in 1983 she became senior vice president/managing broker.

In 1988, Jenny founded Jenny Pruitt & Associates, Realtors, building the company around a "servant spirit." In each of the company's six offices, a director of first impressions ensures that every client is given the company's signature service.

Jenny's accolades include being inducted into the Georgia State Business Hall of Fame; receiving the Lifetime Achievement Award from the Atlanta Business Chronicle and the Honorary Alumni Award from Georgia State University; being inducted into the YWCA 2004 Academy of Women Achievers; and being named one of the 100 Most Influential Georgians.

GENUINE
Southern hospitality

company
Jenny Pruitt & Associates, Realtors

title
Founder and CEO

years in business: 35 total,
16 with Jenny Pruitt & Associates

area of expertise
Residential real estate in the
Atlanta metropolitan area

interests
Community events and projects,
painting, reading, walking

[OPPOSITE] The living room in a totally renovated home by Bill Baker [TOP LEFT] The state-of-the-art kitchen in an award-winning home, Stonehaven Manor [TOP RIGHT] An elegant custom-built stone English Manor estate situated in total privacy in Country Club of the South

[ABOVE] A traditional stucco estate at the end of private cul-de-sac on Garmon Drive
[MIDDLE RIGHT] The media room in Stonehaven Manor [BOTTOM RIGHT] The two-story foyer with sweeping curved staircase and black marble floors in a Garmon Drive estate

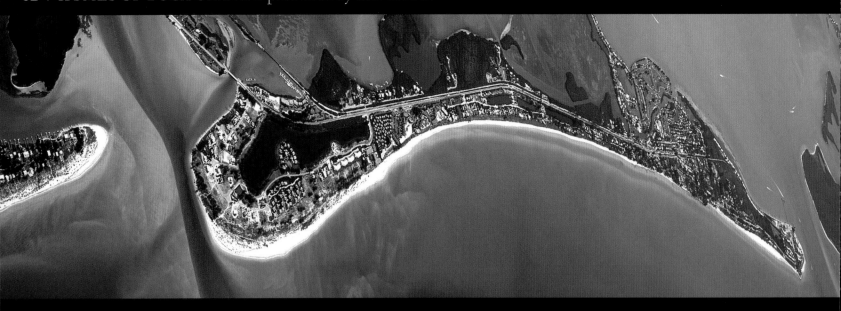

*L*OCATED ON GASPARILLA ISLAND, BOCA GRANDE IS ONE OF THE MOST BEAUTIFUL BARRIER ISLANDS ON FLORIDA'S GULF COAST. Spending time in Boca Grande leaves visitors feeling as if they have stepped back in time, as there are no high-rise condominium developments to spoil the area's Old Florida charm. Boca Grande rests midway between Ft. Myers and Sarasota on the Southwest Coast of Florida. Real estate prices range from around $500,000 to $15,000,000 or more.

GASPARILLA PROPERTIES

Gasparilla Properties is the Boca Grande area's No. 1 real estate sales organization. The company is owned and managed by five partners with decades of real estate experience. Gasparilla Properties specializes in comfortable island area luxury beach and bayfront residential, multi-family and land sales and is the premier company for new construction sales in the region. Additional services include vacation accommodations, area commercial sales, consulting and all other real estate-related services.

GASPARILLA PROPERTIES
411 Park Avenue, P.O. Box 1364
Boca Grande, FL 33921

TEL | 941.964.5650
FAX | 941.964.5654
E-MAIL | bob@gasparillaproperties.com
WEB SITE | www.gasparillaproperties.com

Bob Melvin
Boca Grande, Florida

About Bob Melvin

Bob has been the real estate sales leader in Boca Grande, Placida and on and around the Cape Haze Peninsula for well over a decade. He came to Boca Grande in 1984 from the Ocean Reef Club in Key Largo, Florida and proceeded to sell most of the condominiums, along with numerous homes and lots, while working in sales through the Boca Grande Club.

Bob has led Gasparilla Properties to the pinnacle in island-area real estate sales since founding the company in 1999. Bob and his Boca Grande partners immediately redeveloped the best historic village corner in Boca Grande into what is now the real estate standard for the region.

Bob is proud to call Southwest Florida home. He gives generously of his time and resources to many local organizations, including the Boca Grande Health Clinic, the Island School, Boca Grande Child Care Center, Gasparilla Island Conservation and Improvement Association, Placida Rotary Club, Englewood Area Y.M.C.A. and the Lemon Bay Conservancy.

OLD FLORIDA
charm

[OPPOSITE] The private Coral Creek Club, which features a Tom Fazio-designed golf course and state-of-the-art jet airport *(coralcreekclub.com)*
[TOP LEFT] Inside one of Boca Grande's finest estate properties [TOP RIGHT] The magnificent deck area outside the home pictured at left

[ABOVE] Home with deepwater dockage overlooking Gasparilla Sound and historic railroad trestle [RIGHT] A spectacular bay-front deepwater location with Gulf beach nearby

*M*IAMI IS ONE OF THE WORLD'S MOST EXCITING MULTICULTURAL CITIES, OFFERING PLENTY OF SUN, SAND AND STYLE. Famous for its golden beaches and lively nightlife, the city is full of interesting attractions, such as the Miracle Mile, the famed shopping region. Miami is made up of many distinct districts, including glitzy South Beach, the waterways of the Miami Islands, historical Coral Gables, posh Coconut Grove and the high-rise condos of Brickell Avenue and Key Biscayne.

ESSLINGER-WOOTEN-MAXWELL INC., REALTORS

Founded in 1964, Esslinger-Wooten-Maxwell Inc., Realtors is a full-service residential and commercial brokerage firm with 14 offices serving South Florida. The company is one of the largest residential real estate firms in the U.S. specializing in luxury real estate. Members of Esslinger-Wooten-Maxwell's multilingual, multicultural staff of 950 are adept at conducting business in 17 languages.

ESSLINGER-WOOTEN-
MAXWELL INC., REALTORS
4689 Ponce de Leon Boulevard, Suite 300
Coral Gables, FL 33146

TEL | 305.661.4003
FAX | 305.668.4132
E-MAIL | aross@miamirealestate.com
WEB SITE | www.miamirealestate.com

Audrey H. Ross
Miami, Florida

About Audrey H. Ross

In 1980, after getting remarried, quitting work to travel with her husband, who had sold his company, and becoming immersed in volunteer work, Audrey realized she missed having a career. Rather than return to her former career as an educator, she earned a real estate license and was hired at Cousins & Associates, Inc. Before long she was regularly dealing in the million-dollar-plus market.

In 1984, Audrey opened her own company, Ross & Associates, which evolved from a commercial brokerage into a full brokerage dealing in luxury properties. In 2000, she sold the company to Esslinger-Wooten-Maxwell and became the company's senior vice president and shareholder. In 2003, Esslinger-Wooten-Maxwell was sold to Berkshire Hathaway and is now a subsidiary of that company.

Audrey has been the top producer for her company every year since 2000, selling as much as $63 million in a single week. From 1999 to 2002, she was voted by Mercedes Benz UK and *International Homes* as the Best American Estate Agent.

PLENTY OF SUN,
sand and style

company
Esslinger-Wooten-Maxwell
Inc., Realtors

title
Senior vice president

years in business: 22

area of expertise
Luxury residential and commercial
real estate

interests
Spending time with family and
friends, travel, tennis

[OPPOSITE] A stylish Key Biscayne apartment [TOP LEFT] A custom-built waterfront estate [TOP RIGHT] A Palladian estate located in the gated community Gables by the Sea

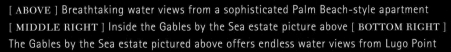

[ABOVE] Breathtaking water views from a sophisticated Palm Beach-style apartment
[MIDDLE RIGHT] Inside the Gables by the Sea estate picture above [BOTTOM RIGHT]
The Gables by the Sea estate pictured above offers endless water views from Lugo Point

$\mathcal{L}$OCATED IN CENTRAL ARIZONA, SCOTTSDALE GETS MORE THAN 300 DAYS OF SUNSHINE A YEAR. Residents of the "Valley of the Sun" enjoy some of the nation's top golf courses, acclaimed restaurants, five major sports teams in new stadiums and a relaxed, unpretentious lifestyle. Low taxes, commanding mountain and fairway views and dramatic rainbow-colored sunsets make Scottsdale a much coveted place to own a home.

REALTY EXECUTIVES/ARIZONA GOLF PROPERTIES AND LUXURY HOMES

Realty Executives has been ranked No. 1 in the sale of luxury properties since 1972. The company first drew attention in the 1960s as the originator of the 100 percent commission concept. Today, phenomenal franchise growth and a unique franchise development strategy continue to generate interest in Realty Executives. The company attracts many of the industry's "elite of the elite" real estate professionals.

**REALTY EXECUTIVES/
ARIZONA GOLF PROPERTIES
AND LUXURY HOMES**
23200 North Pima Road #200
Scottsdale, AZ 85255

TEL | 480.488.4224
FAX | 480.473.1521
E-MAIL | jbgolfhome@aol.com
WEB SITE | www.bradleygolfproperties.com

Joanne Bradley
Scottsdale, Arizona

About Joanne Bradley

Joanne decided to make real estate her career as a single mom in her 20s with two small children. The opportunity to determine when and how much she wanted to work made real estate an ideal career. Successful from the beginning, Joanne was soon hired to start a land department for an Arizona real estate firm. With 12 agents working for her, she gained invaluable experience.

Joanne eventually moved to Realty Executives, where she remains today specializing in exclusive properties, including golf developments.

Joanne is ranked in the top 1 percent of Realty Executives agents and has been named one of the top three agents in Arizona by *Ranking Arizona* magazine every year since the publication's inception in 2000. An avid golfer and travel enthusiast, she has undergone two kidney transplants—a constant reminder to "enjoy the moment, relish my friends, love my family and take nothing for granted as it may not be there tomorrow."

Richard Le Poidevin (left), Joanne Bradley (middle) and Patty Shannon

A RELAXED,
unpretentious lifestyle

company
Realty Executives/Arizona Golf
Properties and Luxury Homes

title
Associate broker

years in business: 30

area of expertise
Scottsdale and surrounding exclusive developments that epitomize

luxury, and concierge services
including golf destinations

interests
Golf, travel, languages (she
speaks Spanish and has studied
French and Japanese), reading,
gourmet cooking classes,
entertaining

[OPPOSITE] Scottsdale offers some of the most exclusive golf developments in the country and a wide range of resort-style amenities [TOP LEFT] Desert Mountain Golf Community, offering six golf courses [TOP RIGHT] A Desert Mountain home on the fairway with breathtaking views

[ABOVE] A rare true adobe home on five acres offering equestrian facilities and dramatic views
[MIDDLE RIGHT] This equestrian retreat with gated entrance includes several fireplaces and spacious rooms for entertaining [BOTTOM RIGHT] Located in Troon Country Club, this south-western Contemporary offers warmth and a private setting with Troon Mountain as its backdrop

DALLAS IS THE THIRD LARGEST AND MOST VISITED CITY IN TEXAS. Dallasites like to live large, and their city reflects this. From the massive Dallas Art Museum to the array of children's activities, the city is a major urban hub boasting an array of interesting attractions. In recent years, various areas of Dallas have been revitalized, including the downtown area, leading to the expansion of the city and an emerging urban lifestyle.

BRIGGS-FREEMAN REAL ESTATE BROKERAGE

Celebrating its rich legacy as the Dallas area's leading boutique firm for premier properties, Briggs-Freeman is proud of its success. The venerable firm is the combination of two of the oldest and most respected real estate companies in the area, which in 1993 merged a common vision, bringing together more than 73 years of experience. Melding traditions of integrity, expertise and a commitment to the client, the partnership has grown into a legend in the community and the entire real estate industry.

**BRIGGS-FREEMAN
REAL ESTATE BROKERAGE**
5600 West Lovers Lane, Suite 224
Dallas, TX 75209

TEL | 800.530.HOME
FAX | 214.350.7503
E-MAIL | rbriggs@briggs-freeman.com
E-MAIL | cfreeman@briggs-freeman.com
WEB SITE | www.briggs-freeman.com

Robbie Briggs & Charles Freeman

Dallas, Texas

About Robbie Briggs & Charles Freeman

A graduate of Tulane University with a master's degree in architecture, Robbie's appreciation of fine homes has served him well since he entered the real estate field in 1980. A leader in the Dallas community, Robbie serves as chairman of the Presbyterian Hospital Foundation. In the past, he has served on the board of directors at The Hockaday School and The Cambridge School of Dallas, as past president of the Juvenile Diabetes Foundation and as a member of the Highland Park Independent School District Dad's Club. He makes his home in Bluffview with his wife, Nancy, and their five children, where they are members of the Park Cities Presbyterian Church.

Since entering the real estate profession in 1964, Charles has achieved national recognition and commanded the respect of other industry leaders as a past director of the Dallas Board of Realtors and former chairman of the Multiple Listing Board. He currently serves on the board of the Juvenile Diabetes Foundation. A fourth-generation Dallasite who resides in University Park, Charles is the father of four children and an active member of St. Michael's Episcopal Church.

Robbie Briggs (left) and Charles Freeman

AN ARRAY OF
interesting attractions

company
Briggs-Freeman Real Estate Brokerage

title
Brokers/co-owners

years in business:
Robbie: 26, Charles: 42

area of expertise
Estate homes/fine properties

interests
Robbie: Traveling China and learning the language

Charles: Windsurfing, fly-fishing and motorcycling

[OPPOSITE] The grand dame of penthouse homes overlooking prestigious Turtle Creek [TOP LEFT] A Dallas gazebo [TOP RIGHT] An incomparable estate home in the historic Kessler Park neighborhood

[ABOVE] A sophisticated Regency-inspired estate in the sought-after Bluffview area
[MIDDLE RIGHT] A soft Contemporary with soaring walls of glass overlooking a serene pool in one of Old Highland Park's most exclusive areas [BOTTOM RIGHT] An example of Dallas's natural beauty

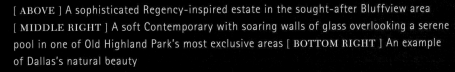

*A*USTIN IS A LITTLE SLICE OF HEAVEN SERVED WITH A HEAVY HELPING OF ONE-OF-A-KIND TEXAS CHARM. The site of the Texas State Capitol, Austin has been nicknamed "Texas's Silicon Valley" because of all the high-tech companies that have migrated there. Within the city limits, one can view historic landmarks, visit top museums, participate in a wide variety of outdoor activities, dine on authentic Texas barbeque and see live music around every corner.

TURNQUIST PARTNERS REALTORS, INC.

Headed by Michele and Steve Turnquist, Turnquist Partners Realtors, Inc. is one of Austin's most dynamic real estate firms, specializing in executive homes, waterfront properties, golf course communities, custom new construction, subdivision lot sales in Austin's most prestigious areas and farm and ranch properties throughout Central Texas. The Turnquist team of experienced professionals prides itself on providing every client with a "can do" attitude and extensive market knowledge.

TURNQUIST PARTNERS REALTORS, INC.
3700 Bee Caves Road
Austin, TX 78746

TEL | 512.328.3939
FAX | 512.328.3922
E-MAIL | m@turnquistpartners.com
WEB SITE | www.turnquistpartners.com

Michele Turnquist
Austin, Texas

About Michele Turnquist

A fourth-generation native Austinite, Michele stems from "Austin Royalty," with a great-grandfather who was the mayor of Austin. She got her start in real estate in 1976 building high-end homes in California, but always knew she would build her career in the city where she was raised.

Today Michele is one of Austin's leading luxury brokers and has achieved a reputation of providing quality real estate service based on integrity, knowledge and professionalism. Thirty years of experience in the industry have taught her that "knowledge is power." She specializes in the sale and marketing of the finest waterfront and luxury estate homes and premier golf course communities, and is the leader in the sale of high-end subdivision lots in the Austin area. Michele is a longtime member of and has served on the advisory board of the Austin Elite 25, which provides a networking arena for top-producing real estate professionals in the high-end market.

ONE-OF-A-KIND
Texas charm

company
Turnquist Partners Realtors, Inc.

title
CEO

years in business: 30

area of expertise
Luxury homes, including waterfront and golf course communities

interests
Wine tasting; the Women's Symphony League of Austin and Helping Hand Home for Children

[OPPOSITE] Working from home Texas-style [TOP LEFT] A stunning Mediterranean-style estate near Lake Travis, just minutes from downtown Austin [TOP RIGHT] A Lake Travis waterfront estate with guest house and boat dock

[ABOVE] A million-dollar view overlooking the Austin hill country [MIDDLE RIGHT] A true Texas wine cellar, a rare find [BOTTOM RIGHT] A Lake Austin waterfront estate in Old Rob Roy

{ WITH ITS AWE-INSPIRING SKYLINE OF ARCHITECTURALLY SIGNIF-
ICANT LANDMARKS, INCLUDING THE GOLDEN GATE BRIDGE,
Trans-America Pyramid Building and Coit Tower, San Francisco is one of the world's
most famous cities. A world leader in technology and an artistic hub, the Bay Area draws
residents from all over the world with its nearby world-renowned wineries, epicurean
delights, mild weather and balanced lifestyle. }

HILL & CO. REAL ESTATE

Hill & Co. Real Estate is the undisputed leader in San Francisco's luxury real estate market, with the highest average price for homes sold in San Francisco every year since 1998. Hill & Co. also boasts a higher percentage of agents with brokers' licenses than any other real estate firm in San Francisco. Celebrating its 50th year in 2006, the company is proud that more than 72 percent of its business comes from repeat customers and referrals.

HILL & CO. REAL ESTATE
1880 Lombard Street
2107 Union Street
San Francisco, CA 94123
WEB SITE | www.Hill-Co.com

TEL | 415.321.4232
FAX | 415.931.9148
E-MAIL | ahlberg1@comcast.net
WEB SITE | www.RealtyInSanFrancisco.com

Stephanie S. Ahlberg
San Francisco, California

About Stephanie S. Ahlberg

A long-time resident of the Bay Area, Stephanie received her B.A. from Sonoma State University and attended graduate school at San Francisco State University. She discovered real estate sales as her husband was starting his medical residency. Her interest was fueled by her family's real estate investments, and once she looked into the industry, she never looked back. Her business took off right away and has continued to flourish through the years. She joined Hill & Co. in 1983.

A top sales leader for years, Stephanie's 2005 sales broke company records for Hill & Co.'s entire 50-year history, earning her distinction as the company's Number One Top Producer! She was also named Outstanding Realtor of the Year for 2005. Stephanie is a founding member of and currently sits as chairperson, advisor or board member on several theater-related organizations. In 2006, she was nominated as Woman of the Year by the San Francisco Leukemia and Lymphoma Society.

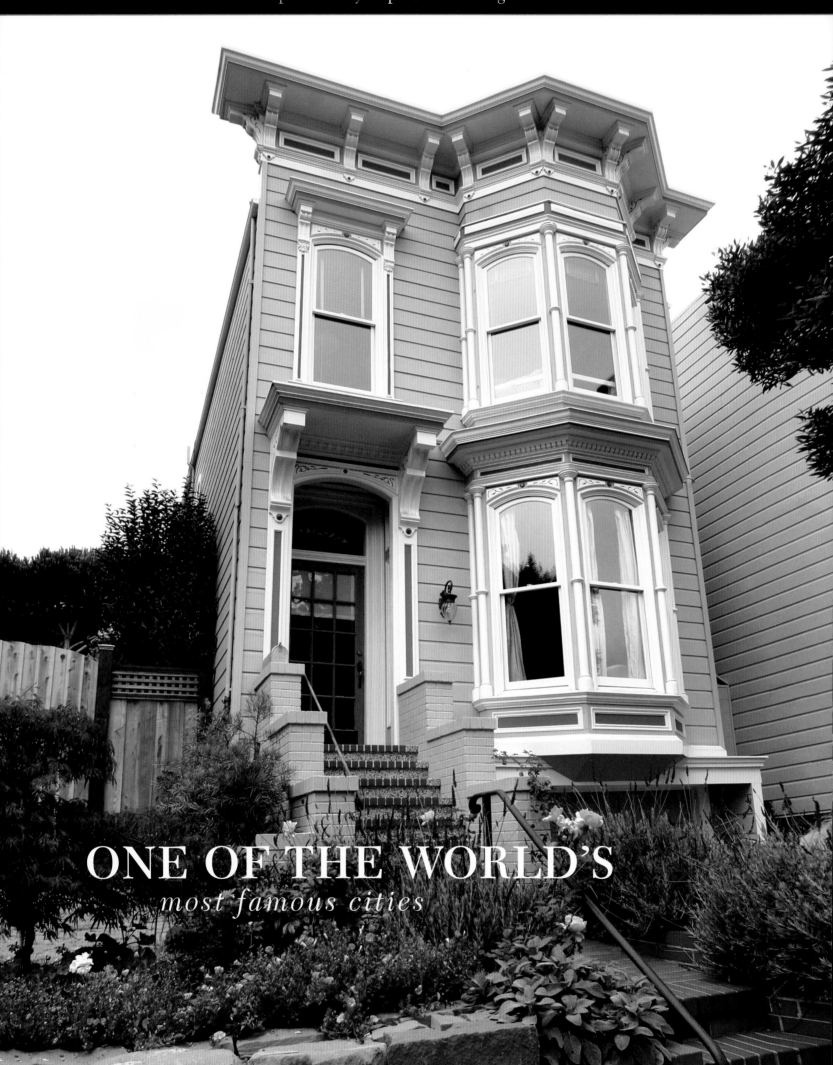

ONE OF THE WORLD'S
most famous cities

company
Hill & Co. Real Estate

title
Broker-associate

years in business: 26

area of expertise
Luxury residential and income properties in San Francisco and Southern Marin

interests
Active participant in theater (both on-stage and through fundraising and membership in theater-related organizations); horse-back riding, cooking, traveling, entertaining and philanthropy

[OPPOSITE] Remodeled and enlarged, this Victorian is one of only a handful of homes registered as part of the Cottage Row Historic District
[TOP LEFT] Enjoy dinner with glistening views of San Francisco Bay [TOP RIGHT] A gracious country estate in southern Marin's beautiful Ross

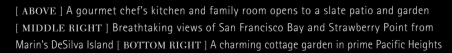

[ABOVE] A gourmet chef's kitchen and family room opens to a slate patio and garden
[MIDDLE RIGHT] Breathtaking views of San Francisco Bay and Strawberry Point from Marin's DeSilva Island [BOTTOM RIGHT] A charming cottage garden in prime Pacific Heights

*C*ORONADO, A SMALL ISLAND TOWN IN SAN DIEGO BAY, IS AN OUT-
DOOR LOVER'S DREAM, with a perfect year-round climate and the most beautiful beaches in Southern California. The world-famous San Diego Zoo, Balboa Park, the
historic Gaslamp District, PETCO Park and the San Diego International Airport are
all less than 15 minutes away. The "Island" is one of the safest places in the U.S., with
nationally recognized schools and a deep sense of community.

SUN ISLE REALTY, INC.

Founded by Scott Aurich in 1989, Sun Isle Realty, Inc. is Coronado's premier independent real estate company. Scott specializes in Coronado and San Diego coastal properties and is joined by eight associates with expertise across San Diego County. While Sun Isle Realty takes great pride in providing quality real estate services for those buying and selling in all price points, Scott has been fortunate to have represented buyers and sellers of some of the most exclusive and prestigious properties in Coronado and La Jolla.

SUN ISLE REALTY, INC.
1339 Orange Avenue, Suite 8
Coronado, CA 92118

TEL | 619.437.1614
FAX | 619.437.1011
E-MAIL | saurich@aol.com
WEB SITE | www.SunIsleRealty.com

Scott Aurich
Coronado, California

About Scott Aurich

Born and raised in Houston, Scott had serious doubts about leaving the Lone Star State. But after visiting Coronado while considering real estate development opportunities in Mexico in the mid-1980s, Scott and his wife, Wanda, and their then 1-year-old son, Scotty, loaded up their truck and moved West. Today selling Coronado as the greatest place on earth comes from Scott's heart.

A past president of the Coronado Association of Realtors, Scott has experience in many different areas of real estate, including the development of single-family subdivisions, custom homes, luxury condominiums and affordable housing. As owner/broker of Sun Isle Realty, Inc., his work is a part of his life that he looks forward to every day.

Scott is a devoted husband to Wanda and father to Scotty. Together they have given their time and money to support the Coronado Schools Foundation, American Cancer Society Relay for Life, Coronado Little League, their church's youth group and many other local organizations and causes.

ISLAND PARADISE
and tropical beauty

All of Coronado's homes are within walking distance of the beach, bay, golf course, yacht club and the world-famous Hotel Del Coronado. They range from the Spreckels Mansion built in 1908 (above left) to luxurious beachfront estates with breathtaking ocean views to quaint cottages on tree-lined, bike-friendly streets

*M*AUI'S SLOGAN IS "MAUI NO KA OI," WHICH MEANS "MAUI IS THE BEST"—AND, ACCORDING TO THOSE LUCKY ENOUGH TO LIVE ON THE VALLEY ISLE, nothing could be closer to the truth. Maui offers arguably the best weather and beaches anywhere in the world. No matter where you are on the island, first-class resort amenities are only a short distance away—ranging from fabulous tennis facilities to glorious golf courses to sophisticated shopping venues.

SAKAMOTO PROPERTIES

Founded by Roy and Betty Sakamoto, Sakamoto Properties specializes in oceanfront and resort properties in the Kapalua, Kaanapali and Wailea resort areas. The dynamic ten-agent firm specializes in high-end properties, but doesn't hesitate to work with first-time homebuyers and diligently help them locate properties that suit their needs. Although the company's agents focus on the residential real estate market, they have also completed a number of commercial transactions over the years. Mitch Mitchell and Dean Otto, both long time associates, complete the professional atmosphere and facilitate the family style operation. They are an integral part of what makes Sakamoto Properties unique.

SAKAMOTO PROPERTIES
5095 Napilihau Street, Suite 203
Lahaina (Napili), Maui, HI 96761

TEL | 808.669.0070
FAX | 808.669.1234
E-MAIL | roy@sakamotoproperties.com
E-MAIL (BETTY) | emailme@maui.net
WEB SITE | www.sakamotoproperties.com
WEB SITE | www.buykapalua.com

Betty & Roy Sakamoto
Maui, Hawaii

About Betty & Roy Sakamoto

Roy, whose grandparents came to Hawaii from Japan, was born and raised in Maui. Betty grew up in Buffalo, New York, and met Roy in 1975 while visiting Maui. The rest, as they say, is history. Betty and Roy have been married for 30 years and established Sakamoto Properties 28 years ago. Since then, the company has become a successful and well-known entity not only in Maui, but throughout the State of Hawaii.

The Sakamotos each chose a career in real estate prior to meeting. Over the years, they have worked with a number of celebrities, as well as international clients. Roy had the honor of being named Realtor of the Year by the Realtors Association of Maui.

Both Betty and Roy have a passion for charity work, including a 20-year commitment to Hale Makua, a Maui non-profit specializing in eldercare. More recently, they pledged their support to a local non-profit school in West Maui, Maui Preparatory Academy. Roy has been named Humanitarian of the Year by the Maui Chamber of Commerce.

THE BEST WEATHER
and beaches in the world

company
Sakamoto Properties

title
Betty: Principal Broker/Vice President

Roy: President

years in business:
60+ combined

area of expertise
The State of Hawaii, specializing in Maui with an emphasis on Kapalua, Kaanapali and ocean-front properties

interests
Their five children and eight grandchildren; golf, tennis and water activities

[OPPOSITE] The Bluest of Blue... [TOP LEFT] Formal living area at 602 Silversword Drive, Kapalua [TOP RIGHT] Fabulous Garden Suite in a tropical setting

[ABOVE] Orchids overhang the pool of this Pineapple Hill home [RIGHT] Exquisite master bedroom overlooking Pacific Ocean

SHANGHAI, CHINA'S LARGEST CITY, CAPTURES ALL THE ENERGY AND EXCITEMENT OF THIS EXOTIC FOREIGN LAND. A port city that draws comparisons to New York City, it is one of the world's most crowded urban areas. Shanghai's 16 million residents enjoy one of China's highest standards of living and are considered to be the country's most cosmopolitan citizens. Shanghai will gain increasing international exposure as it prepares to host the World Expo in 2010.

SHESHAN INTERNATIONAL GOLF CLUB

Spanning 360 acres, it includes an 18-hole, par 72 championship golf course; an 85-acre Tuscan-style village with 116 villas and 118 townhouses designed by acclaimed architecture firm Bassenian & Lagoni; and a golf academy, clubhouse and community center. Residents and guests enjoy the finest hotel-style amenities and accommodations.

SHESHAN INTERNATIONAL GOLF CLUB
No. 288 Linyinxin Avenue
Sheshan National Tourism Resort
Shanghai, 201602, China

TEL | 8621 57655765
FAX | 8621 57657288
E-MAIL | wangcong@sheshangolf.com
WEB SITE | www.sheshangolf.com

Richard Cheung
Shanghai, China

About Richard Cheung

Richard Cheung has been involved in real estate development, commerce and leisure and holiday services since the 1990s. Today he is president of Unifront Enterprise Development Co., Ltd. and chairman of Shanghai Sheshan Golf Club Co., Ltd., the firm behind Sheshan International Golf Club.

Invested by Hong Kong financial consortiums, Uniform Enterprise Development Co. places its focus in real estate development in residence and commercial venues and tour and holiday services.

Unifront has successfully developed projects in Zhejiang, Shanghai and Jilin.

Richard enjoys his work for many reasons, including coordinating the positioning, planning, and design processes, conducting the market survey analysis and implementing the sales plan. It is his philosophy that culture is closely tied to life, and that a real estate project should be the embodiment of culture in a comprehensive, artistic and practical way.

ONE OF CHINA'S
highest standards of living

company
Unifront Enterprise Development
Co., Ltd. and Shanghai Sheshan
Golf Club Co., Ltd.

title
President of Unifront Enterprise Development Co., Ltd. and
chairman of Shanghai Sheshan
International Golf Co., Ltd.

years in business:
Has been involved in his present
line of work since the 1990s

area of expertise
Real estate development, commerce
and leisure and holiday services

interests
Promoting a harmonious way
of life

[OPPOSITE] Night view of a French-style villa with its private swimming pool [TOP LEFT] A French-style villa with its private swimming pool
[TOP RIGHT] A living room with golf course view

[ABOVE] Toscana-style Golf Club house viewed from the green of hole 2
[MIDDLE RIGHT] Toscana-style villa [BOTTOM RIGHT] A Toscana-style dining room

ANCOUVER, CANADA'S THIRD-LARGEST CITY, IS IDEALLY LOCATED IN THE PROVINCE OF BRITISH COLUMBIA. The vibrant international destination is surrounded by water on three sides and overlooks the Coast Mountain Range, which rises dramatically to more than 1,600 feet. Vancouver's two-million-plus residents enjoy one of the mildest climates in Canada. In 2010, Vancouver and nearby Whistler will host the Olympic and Paralympic Winter Games, generating world-wide interest in the area.

CASCADIA PACIFIC REALTY LTD.

Cascadia Pacific Realty Ltd. offers a complete range of exclusive real estate services, including water-front, recreational and resort properties in the Canadian Pacific Northwest. The company has selected a small boutique format to provide quality, one-on-one service to its clients. Whether a client is considering an island retreat, a state-of-the-art oceanfront estate, a downtown penthouse or the sale of an investment, Cascadia's full-service team professionally and expertly meets his or her needs.

CASCADIA PACIFIC REALTY LTD.
1500 West Georgia Street, Suite 1020
Vancouver, BC V6G 2Z6

TEL | 604.638.1802
FAX | 604.638.1809
E-MAIL | irv@cascadiarealty.ca
E-MAIL | beverley@cascadiarealty.ca
WEB SITE | www.cascadiarealty.ca

Irv Ridd & Beverley Kniffen

Vancouver, British Columbia

About Irv Ridd & Beverley Kniffen

As CEO of Cascadia, Irv contributes a wealth of management and sales experience and a comprehensive understanding of his area's real estate market. He has a background in commercial real estate and was formerly employed at one of Canada's largest commercial real estate firms, where he developed the company's Unique Properties Division, now a multimillion-dollar enterprise.

Beverley, Cascadia's president, got her start in real estate at Colliers International, and then continued her successful career with the Shopping Centre division of TrizecHahn Corporation. From there, she progressed into the world of high-end recreational real estate and today is responsible for the sale of some of Vancouver's most highly coveted properties.

Together, Irv and Beverley operate a scholarship foundation that supports students from the Queen Charlotte Islands with a fully funded four-year scholarship to The University of Hawaii or Hawaiian Pacific University.

A VIBRANT
international destination

company
Cascadia Pacific Realty Ltd.

title
Irv is CEO, Beverley is President

years in business:
Irv 25+ years, Beverley 15+ years

area of expertise
Irv: Specialty properties throughout British Columbia, including

ranches, resorts, fishing lodges and retreats

Beverley: Downtown Vancouver luxury properties and waterfront properties in the Gulf Islands

interests
Irv: Fishing, especially salmon fishing in the Queen Charlotte Islands

Beverley: Her horse; she spends her spare time riding in the mountains outside the city of Vancouver

[OPPOSITE] Downtown Vancouver Condominium with fantastic views [TOP LEFT] Oceanfront architectural designed home on Galiano Island
[TOP RIGHT] Living room of Galiano Island home pictured left

[ABOVE] Beautiful bedroom with views of downtown Vancouver [RIGHT] Timber frame
7,000 square foot home

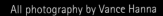
All photography by Vance Hanna

{ THE BAHAMAS, A 100,000-SQUARE-MILE ARCHIPELAGO COMPRISED OF APPROXIMATELY 700 ISLANDS, offers a unique blend of British Colonial architecture and tradition and Caribbean spice. Besides the obvious benefits of flawless weather, pristine beaches and some of the world's clearest water, The Bahamas offers a favorable tax environment, political stability, friendly people and a variety of lifestyle choices, including world-renowned residential communities and premier restaurants and hotels. }

BAHAMAS REALTY LIMITED

Established in 1949, Bahamas Realty Limited is one of the largest and most respected real estate companies in The Bahamas, with a portfolio that includes vacation homes, estate homes, condominiums, commercial holdings, resort properties, acreage and private islands. Their experienced team specializes in working with international buyers and offshore companies who wish to take advantage of The Bahamas' attractive tax-free status.

BAHAMAS REALTY LIMITED
P.O. Box N-1132
Nassau, The Bahamas

TEL | 242.393.8618
FAX | 242.393.0326
E-MAIL | lroberts@bahamasrealty.bs
E-MAIL | mcarey@bahamasrealty.bs
WEB SITE | www.bahamasrealty.bs

Larry Roberts & Mario Carey
The Bahamas

About Larry Roberts & Mario Carey

Born and raised in The Bahamas, Larry attended prep school in Canada and then Rollins College in Florida. After his education, he returned to The Bahamas to pursue a career in real estate, following in the footsteps of his father, Bert Roberts, a pioneer of real estate in The Bahamas. When Larry's father died tragically at the age of 47, he left a legacy that Larry has been able to nurture and grow through Bahamas Realty Limited. Larry is a past president of The Bahamas Real Estate Association, a position he is preparing to resume.

Mario, a native Bahamian, attended high school and college in the U.S. before the ease of living and great weather drew him back home. Both his father and grandfather worked in real estate, and after earning his B.S. from Florida State University, Mario began his own career in real estate, obtaining his training in the U.S. For the past 15 years, Mario has been a top sales producer in The Bahamas. He has the distinction of being the first licensed Bahamian real estate broker to hold both the CRS and CIPS designations.

Mario Carey (left) and Larry Roberts

SOME OF THE WORLD'S
clearest water

[OPPOSITE] Musha Cay, an exclusive island resort in the Exuma Cays [TOP LEFT] Prime beachfront in Ocean Club Estates on Paradise Island
[TOP RIGHT] View from the second-floor balcony of Fairview, a magnificent beachfront estate on Goodman's Bay

[ABOVE] A luxurious harbor-front estate in Ocean Club Estates on Paradise Island
[MIDDLE RIGHT] Island-style elegance in the master bedroom of Creek House on Old
Fort Bay [BOTTOM RIGHT] The beachfront pool and patio of Grange House on Port
New Providence